STEPHEN SPEIGHT

THE FJORD MURDER

Illustrations: Jette Jørgensen

Stephen Speight:
The Fjord Murder
Teen Readers, Level 2

Series editors: Ulla Malmmose
and Charlotte Bistrup

Editorial consultants:
Margaret Kersten
Catherine Candea
Annemarie Zinck

© 1992 by Stephen Speight and
EASY READERS, Copenhagen
- a subsidiary of Lindhardt og Ringhof Forlag A/S,
an Egmont company.

ISBN Denmark 978-87-23-90042-5
www.easyreaders.eu

The CEFR levels stated on the back of the book
are approximate levels.

Easy Readers

EGMONT

Printed in Denmark by
Sangill Grafisk, Holme-Olstrup

About the author

Stephen Speight studied English at Oxford, where he met his future wife. After several years of teaching in comprehensive schools he moved to Edge Hill College of Education. From there he was invited to take up a post in a new English Department in Dortmund, Germany. He has been at Dortmund University ever since, teaching language, literature and technical English, and supervising students on teaching practice. He began work on readers and textbooks soon after arriving in Germany, and has now been working more or less continuously as an educational author for the best part of twenty years. This work has included the script for a German schools' TV series. He contributes regularly to the periodical **Praxis des neusprachlichen Unterrichts**, for which he writes a column called 'Would you have marked it wrong?'. He also lectures and publishes articles on second language conversation, which was the topic of his dissertation. Other professional and leisure interests include modern fiction, life in Britain, caravanning, sailing, jogging and playing the harpsichord.

1. On the *dangerous path*

The man and the woman walked slowly along the path together. It was very beautiful up there, high above the deep, blue water of the *fjord*. The path went in and out of the trees. There were no roads near, no houses, no boats down on the water.

The man and the woman stopped.

"Isn't it *quiet* here," the woman said. She moved her foot on the sand of the path. The small sound *seemed* very loud.

"Yes," the man said. "Too quiet for me. I like to know that other people are near."

"But this walk was your idea. I wanted to look at the town this afternoon."

"We can look at the town tomorrow," the man said. "It was so beautiful today I just had to go and look at the fjord."

"Hmm. That's not like you. I always want to stop and look at things. You want to get there. I want to go for a walk, you want to read the newspaper. But today **you** wanted to go for a walk. Funny! Let me have the camera. I must take a photo of you out for a walk."

The man pulled his heavy camera bag away from her.

---

dangerous, Don't drive so fast. It's dangerous!
path, something to walk along, like a road but smaller
fjord, an arm of the sea in Norway
quiet, there isn't a sound
to seem, if something seems loud, you think it is loud (perhaps it isn't really loud)

"No. You can't take a photo up here. The light isn't right."

* * *

The man and the woman walked on. Soon they were in the trees. The path was *narrow*, and then the rock went straight down to the water more than 100m. below. They stopped again.

"I'm a bit worried," the woman said. "Perhaps it **is** too quiet here. Let's go back."

"No," the man said. "Wait."

"But why? I don't like it up here."

"Why not?"

"I don't know, really. Just a *funny feeling*. Here we are, the two of us. No one else for miles. We could fall in the fjord and no one would ever know."

"Yes, they would. They would find the car. Then they would look for us."

The woman looked at her *husband*. "So you've thought about it!"

"Thought about what?"

"You've thought that you could push me down there, and *get away with* it. *I bet* you'd like to. I know you want to leave me. No one has seen the car. You could get in and drive away – but how about the hotel? Both our names are in their book."

---

narrow, a path is narrower than a road
funny feeling, if you have a funny feeling about something, you are worried about it
husband, Mr Smith is Mrs Smith's husband
to get away with, if you get away with something, no one finds out that you did it
I bet, I think, I just know

"You forget, darling. That was the night before last. And I wrote our names in the book 'Mr and Mrs Smith'! Last night we slept in one of those little *cabins* on a camping site. And this morning we have driven more than two hundred kilometres. No one has any idea where we are. We got there very late, and left early. Perhaps I only put down one name – not my real name, of course."

"But I wrote some postcards this morning."

"You didn't post them. They're still in the car. I could throw them away."

Now the woman was very worried.

"Is this a game? Or have you really planned to *murder* me?"

"No, Jean, it isn't a game." He pulled his wife to the edge of the path, *tied* his heavy camera bag round her, then pushed. She fell, down through the trees, down past the rock and into the water.

* * *

The man looked at the path. He moved the sand a bit with his foot. Then he looked right, left, up and down. No one. He walked slowly back along the path.

* * *

The two children in the small boat did not move. The boat was right in next to the rock. You couldn't see

---

cabins, small huts made of wood where you can stay the night
to murder, to kill
to tie, can you tie these two ends together?

7

it from the path. The children didn't know what had happened up there. But they did hear something. They heard the name Jean, and something about postcards. Then there was a *splash* and they saw the woman go under.

For a few seconds the children were too *shocked* to say anything. They just sat in their boat and looked at the place where the woman had gone down.

She didn't come up again. But something else did. A little black plastic film box. The boy picked it up and *shook* it. Then he opened it. There was a film in it.

The girl *came back to life*.
"That poor woman!" she said. "We must try to help her."
She started to pull her shoes off.
"No don't," the boy said. "It's *terrible*, but we can't do anything. I'm sure the fjord is hundreds of feet deep here."
"We must do something!" the girl said.
"The best thing we can do is go to the police, and tell them a woman has fallen in the fjord. Perhaps they'll

---

splash, the sound something makes when it falls in the water
shocked, after an accident people are often shocked. They can't move or do anything for a while
shook, past tense of to shake. To move something quickly from side to side or up and down
to come back to life, to feel better, start to move and speak again after a shock
terrible, very bad

believe us and come and look for her."

"But if you're right, they won't find her, and they'll think it's just a silly story. Let's go back to the camping site and try to forget all about it."

"Can you forget what we saw?" the boy asked.

"No, of course not."

"Perhaps she fell," the boy said slowly, "and perhaps she was pushed. If she was pushed it was murder! And the murderer was just up there on the path. Let's go back. Perhaps the police can *catch* him."

"We can't go back yet," the girl said. "Perhaps she **will** come up again. Perhaps she isn't *dead*."

"She **is** dead," the boy said. "Didn't you see? There was a bag, a heavy camera bag. It was tied round her. She can't come up again. She will never come up again. Not in a hundred years."

---

to believe, to think something really happened or is *true* (*true*, not just a story)
to catch, you can catch a ball and the police try to catch murderers
dead, I think your hamster is dead. It hasn't moved for three days

2. Broken grass and a bit of wool

The children *paddled* their little boat back to the camping site. They were Paul and Jackie Robinson, on holiday in Norway with their parents. Paul and Jackie didn't say very much on the way back. Their parents ran down to the water when they saw them.

"Hello, kids. Did you have some fun in the boat?" their father asked.

Then he saw their faces.

"What's the matter? There's nothing wrong, is there?"

They told their story. When the story was finished, it was very quiet down there by the fjord.

"We must go to the police," the mother said. "We can ask that nice Norwegian family to help us."

They carried the boat back up to their tent, then went over to the Norwegian caravan. The Melings were just having a cup of coffee.

"Come in," they said, through the open window.

They all sat round the table, and the children told their story again.

Mrs Meling looked at them hard.

"All this really happened?" she asked.

"Yes, really."

"Then we'll take you to the police station in the village."

---

to paddle, this is a paddle, you can use it to paddle a boat

Mr and Mrs Meling went over to their Saab. Paul and Jackie got into the back. The Melings' dog jumped in with them.

* * *

The Norwegian policeman listened to the story, too. His English wasn't very good, so the Melings helped to explain everything.

The policeman was a man of few words. At the end of the story he got up.

"Come with me," he said.

The Norwegians and the English children got into the police car and the dog jumped in, too. The policeman drove out along the fjord. After a few miles he stopped.

"Here the road turns left and goes into the *mountains*. There's a path along the fjord. It begins over there."

The boy, Paul, looked down at the fjord.

"Yes, we went along there in our boat," he said. "And the murderer must have left his car just here."

"Hmm," the policeman said. He got out of his car and walked round the little car park at the start of the path. He looked at the sand and grass.

"A lot of cars," he said, then, "Come with me."

* * *

They all walked along the little path, in and out of the trees. The dog ran on in front of them. Paul looked down at the fjord.

"What do you think, Jackie?" he said to his sister. "Is this the right place?"

---

mountain, a very big hill

"No – it was further along."

Suddenly the dog stopped at the edge of the path and barked.

"What is it, boy?" Mr Meling asked. Everybody ran to see what the dog was looking at. There was nothing to see. "Hmm," the policeman said again. He ran his hand over the grass at the side of the path. "Broken grass," he said. "It's not much ..."

"Look," Paul said. "A bit of blue wool down there on that bush."

"Was the woman wearing something blue?" Mrs Meling asked.

"Yes, a blue pullover," Jackie said.

"Hold my feet," Paul said. "I want to get that bit of wool."

The policeman and the Norwegian held Paul's feet. He could just get the bit of wool. They pulled him back on to the path.

"You do believe us, don't you?" Jackie said to the policeman.

"Yes, I think so. Let me have the wool, please. It could be important."

Paul gave him the wool but he pulled off a little piece first.

"Will you look for the *body* in the fjord?" he asked.

"We will look but we will not find it," the policeman said.

They walked back along the path together. Paul put his hand in his *pocket*, opened the little black box, and put the piece of wool in with the film.

---

body, a dead person
pocket, jeans have pockets at the sides, and at the back

3. The film

Paul did not sleep that night. As soon as the shops opened he ran into town with the film. He found a shop with a sign in the window in English: *SAME DAY SERVICE*. He gave in his film, but he kept the little black box, and the piece of blue wool.

The girl in the shop said his pictures would be ready at about four in the afternoon. It was a very long day for Paul. He thought four o'clock would never come. He went out in the boat with his sister for an hour or two, but he was very quiet.

"Come on, Paul," his sister said. "We can't do anything. Try to think of other things."

"I'm trying, but I can't. I'm sure there's a murderer somewhere near here. I want to get him!"

"That's silly, Paul. Perhaps the woman just fell."

"No, she didn't. That heavy camera bag – it was tied round her."

"Well, yes, you're right there. But you don't know where to start."

"Perhaps I do. Remember that film?"

"Paul! You didn't give it to the police. Where is it?"

"I took it in. I can get the pictures at four o'clock this afternoon. Do you want to come with me?"

"Yes, of course."

* * *

The children sat outside a small café in the sun. Paul

---

same day service, if you take your film in in the morning, you get your photos back before the shop closes in the evening

took out the pictures. They looked at them one by one. Most of them showed fjords, mountains, old wooden houses. But two of the pictures were more interesting.

One showed a woman. She was on a *ferry*, and you couldn't see her face. But she was wearing a blue pullover.

"That's her!" Paul said. They looked at the photo of the dead woman. It was a funny feeling.

The other interesting photo showed a Norwegian *stave church*, with cars outside it.

"Hey," Jackie said. "That's Borgund stave church. We went there last week."

Two of the cars on the photo were English. A family was getting into one of the cars, but the other one was empty.

"That white Escort could be the murderer's car!" Paul said, "and I can read the number!"

"Just a second," Jackie said. "How do you know he's English?"

"Oh!" Paul said. "That's a very good question. Yes, of course. We heard a bit of English from up there on the path."

"That's right. She said something about postcards, and he called her Jean. But there's something else. The murderer wouldn't take a photo with his car in it. It would be dangerous for him."

"Perhaps he was in the church," Paul said, "and his *wife* took the photo. Perhaps he doesn't know this photo

---

ferry, a big boat (ship) which takes people (often cars, too) across a river, fjord, etc.
stave church, a very old wooden church in Norway
wife, Mr and Mrs Smith are husband and wife

is on the film."

"Hmm. You could be right," Jackie said. "But he took a photo of his wife!"

"Yes, but you can't see her face!"

"Okay, but we don't **know** the Escort is his. Perhaps he was standing by his car and it isn't in the picture!"

"Okay, okay, but I have this feeling about the Escort."

They didn't say anything for a while. Then Jackie had an idea.

"Look," she said, "we've got a photo of the dead woman, and we think we've got a photo of the murderer's car. Let's show them to the policeman. He can check that car number. You know, there's that place in Swansea where they keep all the information about British cars."

* * *

The Norwegian policeman looked at the photos.

"And you think this is the murderer's car," he said slowly.

"Well, it **could** be," Paul said.

"Okay, I'll check the number."

He gave the children a hard look.

"I know you're interested in this murder," he said. "You saw it! But from now on it's police work, okay? Murderers are dangerous people!"

"But you could tell us what you find out," Jackie said.

"Well, all right. It will take a little while – they'll do the check from Oslo. You could come in tomorrow morning. Perhaps there'll be some news by then."

4. The car

While the police were checking the car number, the murderer was driving, driving, hundreds of miles. Somewhere on the way he bought petrol and threw away his wife's things. He slept in the car, somewhere where no one could see him. Next morning he bought a newspaper and something to eat. It was his first meal since the murder. He looked at the newspaper. He couldn't read Norwegian, but there could be a photo of the body ... Of course there was nothing about his wife. She was under hundreds of metres of water. He was quite *safe*. No one was looking for him.

* * *

He drove on more slowly. He had to plan things. He went through the plan so far in his head. His wife's name was not on the ferry tickets. There was just his name plus "1 person". They had left home very early in the morning. None of the *neighbours* was up. The passport officer had looked into the car at Dover. Would the man remember his wife's face? No. *Not a chance*.

The murderer had crossed to France and then driven to Norway. He was planning to drive back the same way, and meet his girlfriend in France. When they went back to England, she would be the "1 person" on his ticket. No need to chance anything. He had told his wife their holiday would be in France. The trip to

---

safe, not in danger
neighbours, people who live in the same street
not a chance, it just can't happen

Norway was a '*special surprise*' for her. No one would ever know about the trip to Norway – or the murder.

Jean's friends would ask questions. He wasn't worried. He could answer them.

"Yes, it's very *sad*. We just don't want to live together any more. I went on holiday with my girlfriend, and Jean, well, she left the same day. She said she wanted to stay with friends."

Everyone knew he and his wife weren't happy together. People would soon stop asking questions.

Perhaps the police would not even ask any questions. He wouldn't tell them she was *missing*. Why should he? He thought she was staying with friends. That was the story, and it was a good one.

* * *

Next morning Paul and Jackie went back to the police station.

"Well," they asked, "What's the news?"

"Sorry," the policeman said. "There isn't any news. There is no English car with that number, so we can't find the driver."

"Oh well," Paul said. "So much for that idea!"

The policeman smiled.

---

special, you need a special film for that old camera
surprise, a nice little 'shock'
sad, not happy
missing, a missing person is someone who has been away from home for a long time. The police and their family don't know where they are.

"But if the number isn't real, there **is** something funny about that car. We think your story could be true."

"You do? Thank you," Paul said. "I know you haven't got any real *clues*."

"No. This murderer is very clever. We've checked the fjord, but it's too deep. We found nothing. Now we've checked the Escort and there's no car with that number. We've also telephoned hotels and camping sites. Nothing! Well, nothing we can use."

"What does that mean?" Paul asked.

"Well, there **was** a white Escort at the Hotel Husum three nights ago. There are thousands and thousands of white Escorts, of course."

"Was this one English?"

"Yes - a Mr and Mrs Smith."

"Smith?" Jackie said. "People write Smith when they don't want to give their real names."

"We have been to the hotel," the policeman said. "The girl at *reception* thought she remembered the faces. But we can't find the man, and the woman . . ."

"Yes, we know," Jackie said.

Paul was thinking.

"This Hotel Husum," he said. "Is it white? An old *building*, very pretty?

"Well, yes," the policeman said.

"We passed it on our way north. It's near Borgund stave church, isn't it, the one on the photo."

---

clues, little things which help the police to catch a murderer
reception, the big desk near the door of a hotel, and the people who work there
building, a house, church etc.

"Have you got the photo with you?" the policeman asked.

"Yes," Paul said. "Here you are."

The policeman looked at it.

"You're right!" he said. "Borgund stave church."

"So there was a white Escort at the church," Paul said, "and at the hotel – 'Mr and Mrs Smith's' Escort. But the car hasn't got a real number. 'Mr Smith' is the murderer. I just know he is!"

"You could be right," the policeman said. "But there's no way we can find him."

5. Too late?

It was near the end of the Robinsons' holiday now. Jackie was trying to forget about the murder, but Paul couldn't forget. He thought about it all the time. He wanted to catch the man, a man he had never seen.

What would the man do? Paul tried to think. He closed his eyes. He saw the man. The man was walking along the path, back to his car. The man got into his car. He saw his wife's postcards, and other things of hers. Her bag was in the back of the car.

"I think he drove a long way," Paul said to himself. "He didn't want to throw anything away near here. But all the time his wife's things worried him. When it got dark, he threw them away. Where? It was the afternoon when he murdered his wife. You can't go very fast on these little roads."

Paul walked over to his parents' car and got out the map of Norway.

"Which way did he go?" Paul thought. "I'm sure he went south. He wanted to get out of the country. He'd think he was okay then." There was only one main road south on the map. Paul ran his finger down the road. "He could get to about **here**," he thought.

His father came over to the car.

"Planning the trip home, Paul?" he asked.

"Well, there's only one main road south from here."

"Let me see," his father said. "Yes, you're right. But *I bet* you were really thinking about that murderer."

I bet, I think, I just know

"Yes. I think he drove down this road, too."

"Hmm. Perhaps he did, perhaps he didn't."

"Dad, can we stop a few times on our way tomorrow. We could talk to people and ask if they've seen a white Escort. Or perhaps the man threw his wife's things away somewhere."

"But Paul, he could just drive off into the forest if he wanted to do that. We'd never find them."

"But we could just stop and ask people, couldn't we? At *filling stations* and camping sites."

"He wouldn't go to a camping site – too dangerous."

"Okay then Dad, just the filling stations. There won't be many on that road. He had to buy petrol somewhere."

* * *

They started for home early the next morning. Mrs Robinson was driving, and Mr Robinson was looking at the map. When they had gone about a hundred and fifty kilometres they stopped at a *garage*.

Paul jumped out of the car and ran across to the office.

"Excuse me," he said to the woman, "We're looking for a man in a white Escort. He's English."

"When did he come past here?"

"We're not sure. Two days ago, we think."

"No, sorry. I'd remember a white Escort from England. He didn't stop here."

Paul ran back to the car.

---

filling station, a place where you can buy petrol (gas) for cars
garage, another word for filling station

"*No luck*. Let's try the next garage."

"Paul," his mother said, "I know you want to catch this murderer, but the chances are so small. Can't we just drive home happily and forget about him?"

"Please, mum."

"Oh well," his mother said, and started the car. "We'll need petrol soon anyway."

* * *

"There's the next garage," Paul shouted.

It was a very small place, with a wooden hut at the back. An old man came out of the hut.

Paul ran across to him.

"Hello," he said, "Do you speak English?"

"Yes," the man said. "And it's a good thing, too."

"How do you mean?"

"Well, I seem to need English more and more these days."

Paul's *heart* began *to beat* faster.

"Have other English cars stopped here, then?"

"Yes, that's what I mean."

Paul tried to speak slowly.

"Was there a white Escort, a day or two ago."

"Yes, there was."

Paul's heart nearly stopped.

"With just a man in it?"

"Oh, you know him, do you?"

---

no luck, I wasn't lucky (someone who wins a lot of money is lucky)
heart, most people draw a heart like this:
to beat, if you run your heart beats faster

"No, but we're looking for him."

"I see. Well, I hope he's not a friend of yours. We were just closing for the night when he stopped here and bought petrol. Said he was in a hurry. Looked back down the road all the time. I thought he was worried about something. But he didn't drive off down the road. He went up there."

The man pointed to a path into the forest. It was *wide* enough for a car.

"Ten minutes later he came back again. And do you know what he did up there?"

"I bet he threw some clothes away," Paul said. "I'll go and look. It could be . . ."

The man stopped him.

"Too late," he said. "But you're right about the clothes. I walked up the path and found them. Women's clothes. And a bag. It was all quite new."

"What did you do with the things?"

"Threw them in the *bins*. We like to keep our country clean. But later I thought . . . "

Paul ran across to the two big bins before the man could stop him. They were both empty.

"Too late again, *I'm afraid*," the man said. "Yesterday was bin day."

Paul just stood there, looking at the two empty bins. A day earlier, and they would have found something really *important*. But now it was too late . . . and then he saw it. Something coloured in the grass between the

---

wide, most roads are wide, most paths are narrow
I'm afraid, (here), I'm sorry
important, I must talk to you. It's really important

bin

bins. He ran across and picked it up. It was part of a postcard, a postcard of a stave church. On the other side you could read part of an address. The town was Bournemouth, but half the street name was missing.

Jackie ran across from the car.
"What have you found, Paul?" she asked.
"It's part of a postcard. It could be a real clue," Paul said.
The two children looked at the piece of postcard together. Paul put the photo of the stave church next to it.
"It's the same church, Borgund," he said. "But we can't read the address.
"Yes, we can," Jackie said. "I once did a puzzle like this. Look, you can take letters from over here, and find

which top halves go with which bottom halves. *I'm sure* we can find the name of the street and the number of the house."

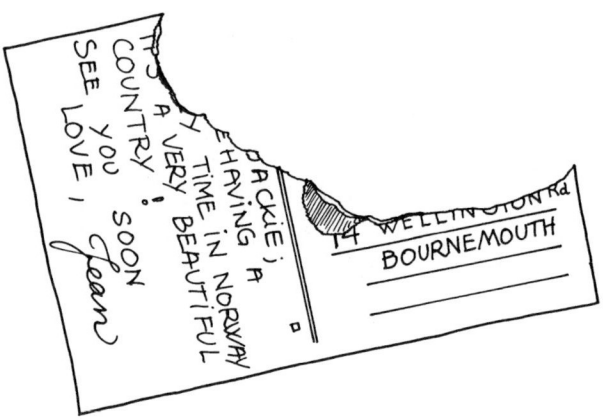

Paul looked at the writing on the left of the card.
"Jackie!" he said. "We're looking at the address and we haven't looked at who wrote the card."

It said, "Love, Jean."

I'm sure, I just know, I bet

6. Going home

The Robinsons drove slowly on down Norway, stopping for a day here and a day there. The murderer was going home, too, but now he was driving fast. And he wasn't going straight back home.

He took the ferry to Denmark, drove into Germany, and on into Holland and Belgium. Somewhere along the Belgian coast he stopped. When it got dark, he put the real number plates back on his car. He didn't throw the other number plates away. They were from his first car, an old *MG Midget*.

No one knew that he, or his car or his wife had been to Norway. He felt better now. He could sleep in the car for a few hours. His girlfriend was crossing the Channel to Calais in two days' time. They would *travel* back on his ticket.

His girlfriend didn't live in Bournemouth. And she wouldn't come and live in his house, not for a long time. After about a year it would be okay. No more questions then. The *perfect* murder. The man closed his eyes and tried to sleep.

* * *

While the murderer was sleeping in his car in Belgium, the Robinsons were in their tent on a camping site near

---

MG Midget, an old British sports car
to travel, to go on a (long) trip
perfect, nothing wrong with something, no mistakes

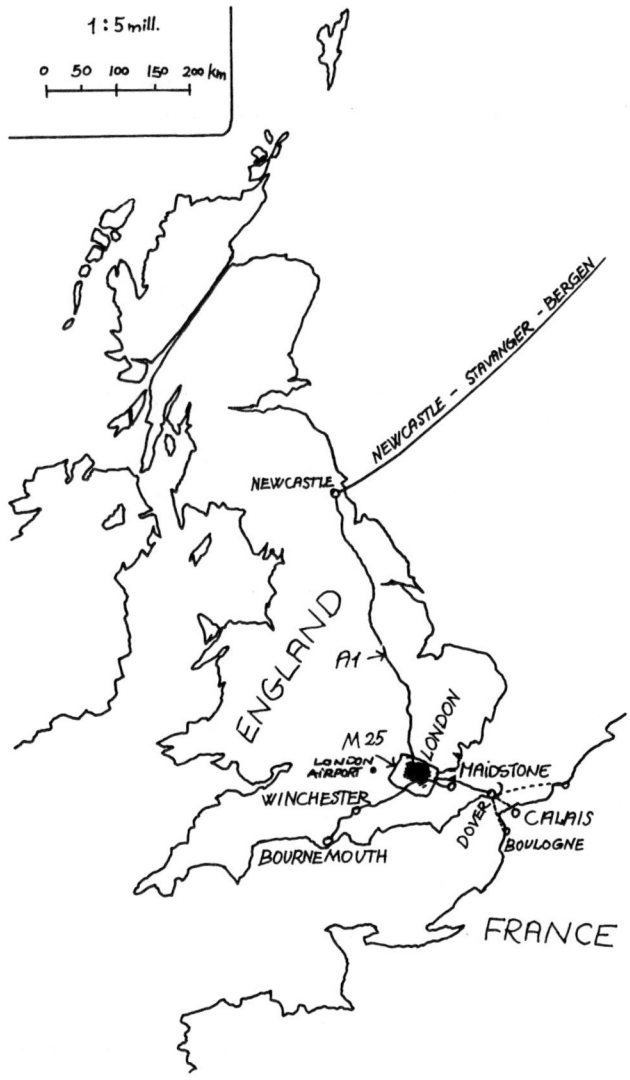

Bergen. They wanted to cross to England the next morning, too. So the murderer and the "detectives" were at sea together in *different* ships.

The Robinsons drove off the ferry and went south. They lived near Maidstone in Kent. The murderer drove off the ferry and into Dover. His girlfriend's car was parked there. They said goodbye. She drove home to Winchester, and he drove home to Bournemouth.

School started for Paul and Jackie the next morning. They had the address of Jean's friend in Bournemouth, and perhaps they could have got her phone number, but they didn't try. It could be dangerous. Perhaps she would tell the murderer. So they waited until the weekend.

"Dad," Paul said on Friday evening, "how about a trip to Bournemouth tomorrow?"

"Sorry. I've got to work in the garden. Just look at it! Three weeks of holiday, and you don't know where to start. I need some help. Perhaps you two ..."

"But Dad," Jackie said, "you know we want to try and catch the murderer."

"Yes, but it could be dangerous. Go and tell the police."

"They'll laugh at us. We need more clues."

Mrs Robinson didn't like gardening very much.

"I'll take you to Bournemouth," she said. "Then I can keep an eye on you – see that you don't do anything silly."

* * *

---

different, not the same

Wellington Road was easy to find. Mrs Robinson stopped the car and the children got out.

"I'll stay in the car," she said. "Call me if you need help."

The children walked along the road. They soon found number 14. Paul went up to the door.

"Well, go on then, ring the bell," Jackie said.

"I'm a bit worried."

"This isn't the murderer's house."

"No, you're right. Okay then."

Paul rang the bell.

A woman came to the door.

"Hello," she said. "Money for the Red Cross or something is it? Just a second. I'll get my bag."

"Er no." Paul said. "We don't want any money."

"*What's the matter?*" the woman said. "You look quite white."

Paul got out the piece of postcard.

"Look," he said. "We think a friend of yours wanted to send you this postcard from Norway."

The woman looked at the card.

"Jean," she said. "Yes, Jean Bishop. We always send one another cards when we're on holiday. But I didn't know she was going to Norway. I think she said France. Where did you get this card, and why is there only a piece of it? I can see you're worried about something. Come in and tell me all about it."

* * *

So the children told their story again. The woman listened.

"Ray Bishop a murderer?" she said at the end. "I can't believe it! And Jean dead? At the bottom of a fjord? These are people I **know**, *ordinary* Bournemouth people like me, well, more or less like me. I never liked Ray very much."

"Murderers **are** ordinary people," Jackie said. "I read that somewhere."

"Hmm," the woman said. "That's a thought! What are you going to do next?"

"We want to go to Ray Bishop's house," Paul said. "Can you give us the address?"

---

what's the matter?, what's wrong?
ordinary, not special

7. Number plates

The children went back to the car.

"Well?" their mother asked, "how did you get on?"

"We've got the murderer's address," Paul said. "His name is Ray Bishop and he lives in Charminster Road. The woman said it was just round the corner from here – down there and turn right."

"Just a minute now," Mrs Robinson said. "If this Ray Bishop **is** a murderer, you can't just go round and ring his bell. We've got to go to the police."

"Can't we just drive past the house?" Jackie asked. "We've followed him all the way from Norway. I want to see where he lives."

"Well, all right," Mrs Robinson said. "I don't think that can be dangerous."

She turned the car round, drove back along Wellington Road and turned right into Charminster Road.

"What was the number again?" she asked.

"A hundred and seventeen," Paul said.

"It must be quite a way along, then," Mrs Robinson said. "This is only fifteen." She drove slowly along the road.

"There it is!" Jackie said. They drove past the house.

"No one's at home," Mrs Robinson said. "He's gone out in the car and left the garage door half open."

The children looked. Then Paul suddenly shouted, "Drive on a bit, then stop, Mum. Please."

Paul jumped out of the car and ran to the garage. He was inside for about half a minute, then he ran out again with something inside his jacket.

"Drive on, Mum, quickly, before anyone sees us."

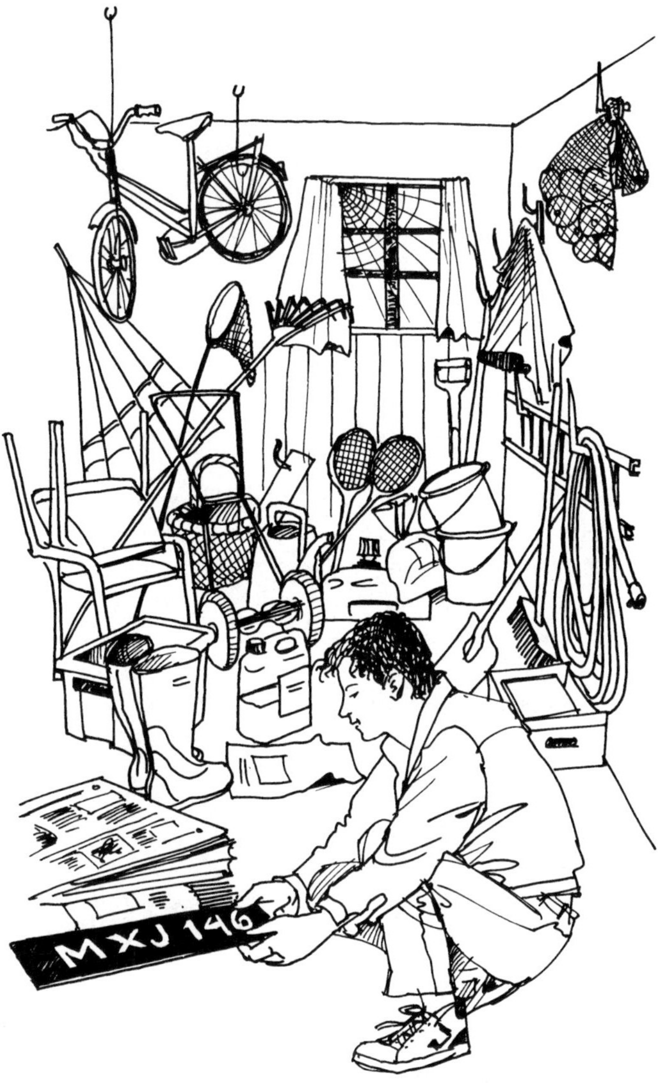
MXJ 146

None of them saw a white Escort turn into the road. It was Ray Bishop's car. He saw Paul run out of his garage and get in the car. He nearly drove after the Robinsons, but then he didn't. He ran across to his garage and looked inside.

"The number plates!" he shouted. "That kid has got the number plates. Why didn't I throw them away?"

He went into the house and telephoned his girlfriend. Then he started to pack.

* * *

Mrs Robinson drove on down the road. "Where do we go next?" she asked.

"To the police station," Paul said. "We've got all the clues we need."

Jackie was sitting in the front. She turned round to her brother.

"What have you got? Show me. I'm in this too, you know."

Paul opened his jacket and took out two number plates.

"That's the number on the photograph!" Jackie said.

"I know. We've got him. I knew we would in the end."

* * *

The policeman listened to *part* of the story, then he said, "Just a second. This is something for the inspector."

---

part, not all of something

In the inspector's office, the children started their story again, and told it right up to that morning in Charminster Road. The inspector made notes.

"Let me just check," he said when they had finished. "You think Ray Bishop is a murderer because
- a woman you think was his wife fell in the fjord
- just before this you heard the name Jean and the word postcard
- you found some blue wool on the path. It was the same colour as Jean Bishop's pullover, which you have seen on a photo
- you also have a photo of a white Escort with Ray Bishop's old number plates on it
- this photo – and the other one – was on a film which you found in the fjord, and it shows a stave church
- you then found part of a postcard with this church on it
- the card was near a dustbin at a filling station on the road south
- the garage man remembered the white Escort
- Ray Bishop had bought petrol there, and thrown away his wife's clothes – the postcard, too, of course
- the postcard was addressed to a friend of Mrs Bishop's
- you could read the address, so you came here today, talked to the friend, and got Mr Bishop's address
- you then went round to his house and *stole* – let's say took the number plates from his garage.
Is that right?"

"Yes," Paul said. "That's the story."

---

stole, past tense of to steal, to take something that isn't yours

"Well done," the detective said. "He's a murderer, and you've helped to catch him. Wait here, please."

"Get me a car!" he shouted as he ran out of his office, "and I need two *officers*."

---

officer, here, a policeman

8. The bird has flown

Ten minutes later the inspector was back again.

"Too late!" he said. "*The bird has flown.*" He picked up the phone.

"We must check all *ports* and airports," he said. "He'll try to get out of the country with his girlfriend, perhaps."

"Girlfriend?" Jackie said. "We don't know anything about a girlfriend."

"But **we** do. We talked to Mrs Bishop's friend. She saw Ray Bishop in town with another woman. And we know something else. Mrs Bishop had *quite a lot* of money." The detective made some telephone calls.

"Excuse me," Mrs Robinson said. "What do we do next?"

"Oh, er, yes," the detective said. "Well, there's nothing more you can do here. You can go home now. When there's some news, we'll let you know."

* * *

"So that's that," Jackie said. "I was so *excited* in Bournemouth. I thought we'd see the murderer at last. I thought the police would catch him."

"They will catch him," Mrs Robinson said. "They know all about him now. His address, his car, his girlfriend ..."

---

the bird has flown, someone you want to catch has got away
ports, towns on the sea where ships come in and go out
quite a lot, more than a bit
excited, it's my birthday tomorrow. I'm so excited

"But we haven't even got a photo of him," Jackie said.

"That's funny isn't it. We've *followed* him all the way to here, but we don't know what he looks like."

* * *

Ray Bishop drove to his girlfriend's house, and then he drove to London airport. They parked the car in one of the big car parks.

"I'm *frightened*," the girlfriend said. "Perhaps they're already looking for us."

"You don't know that."

"No, but why would that kid take the old number plates from your garage?"

"That's why we're getting out. We can *start a new life* with Jean's money."

"You haven't got it yet!"

"No, of course not. But it's mine now. And so is the house."

"Ours, you mean," the girl said coldly.

"Yes, of course. Ours." Ray said quickly.

"Where are we going?" the girl asked.

"Somewhere they don't ask questions. I was thinking of South America."

"Why not Rio? No one will find us there."

"Okay. Rio it is."

They went to *book* their *flight*. It took quite a long

---

to follow, to go after
frightened, are you frightened of big dogs?
to start a new life, to go somewhere else and make a new start
to book, to buy a ticket for something
flight, a trip in a plane

time, and they were getting more and more *nervous*. They sat in a cafeteria waiting for their flight. Now and then there was something on the loudspeakers. But no one was asking for a Mr Bishop. They began to feel a bit better. At last their flight was called. They got up and walked to the passport check. There was a long line of people.

"Come on, come on!" Ray said to himself. "Let's get through here and onto the plane."

At last! Ray handed his passport to the man at the desk.

* * *

There were two passport officers.

"He looks a bit nervous," one said to the other.

"Take your time. Let him wait a bit. Go through the list very slowly."

"We've got a Bishop here, but the name is Vincent Bishop."

"No, Vincent Bishop is a terrorist. I've seen a photo."

"Okay, then. Let him go. Perhaps he's just running away from his wife ..."

The two men laughed.

At that moment Ray **did** run. He *grabbed* his passport and ran out, along the *corridors*, and out to the plane. The two passport officers followed him and so did an airport policeman. They got him half way across to the plane.

---

nervous, worried and *jumpy*. *Jumpy*, you jump at every little sound
to grab, to take something quickly
corridor, if you look along the corridor, you will see the doors to the offices on each side

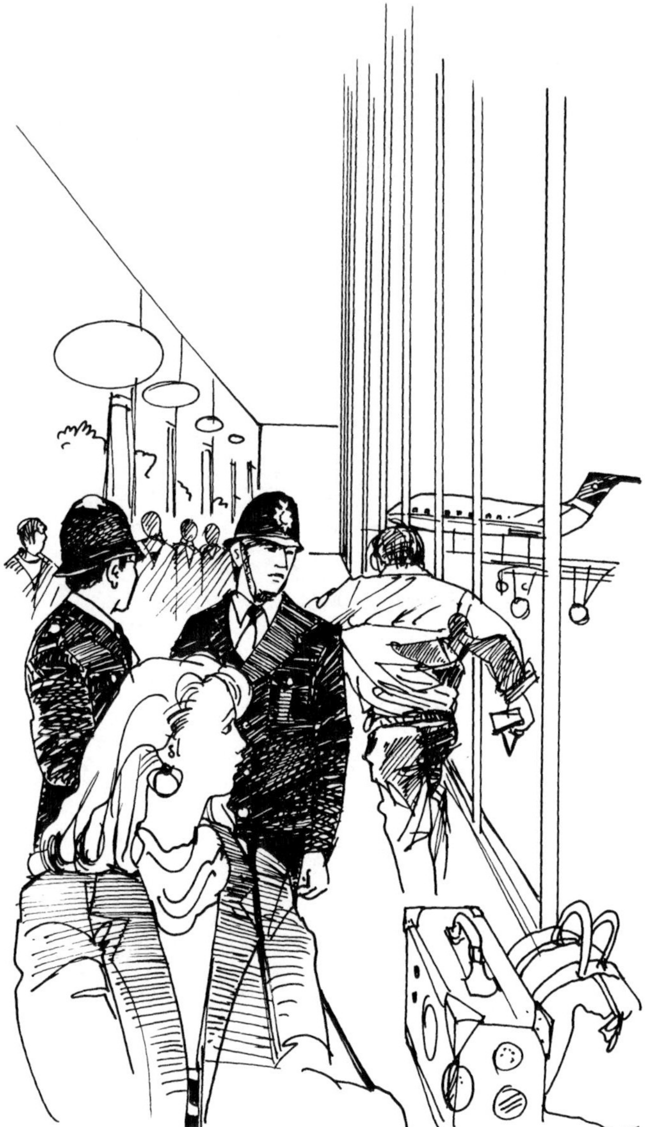

"Why did he run away?" the policeman asked.

"We don't know. We took our time with his passport because he looked a bit nervous ..."

"You don't know?" Bishop said. "You mean I wasn't on that list of names?"

"No. There's a Vincent Bishop on the list, but we know you're not him."

"Bishop?" the policeman said. "I've just had a call about a Mr Bishop, Ray Bishop. I was on my way to tell you. They think he murdered his wife."

9. Blue wool

Not long after the Robinsons got home, the telephone rang. Mr Robinson took the call. It was the police. They had caught Ray Bishop at London Airport, and they wanted to talk to the children. There were still a few more questions.

So Mrs Robinson got the car out again, and drove the children round the *M25* to London Airport. A young policeman was waiting for them.

"You can park the car over there. Then come with me, please."

Bishop was sitting on one side of a desk, and an inspector from Scotland Yard was on the other side.

"Ah!" he said. "The young detectives."

Bishop turned round. "How did you find out?"

"We were in a little boat," Paul said. "We saw your wife fall in the fjord. There was a film. Perhaps it was in that bag, the heavy camera bag you tied round her."

"I must have missed it. I took my camera *stuff* out and filled the bag with stones that morning. But I never photographed the car. I knew that was dangerous."

"We think your wife took the photo."

"Yes, she must have done. I went on to the church, and she came later. So Jean *ruined* my perfect murder. I kept the plates from my dear old MG – silly of me."

M25, the motorway (a very big road) round London
stuff, a word you can use for nearly anything: sports stuff, camera stuff, swimming stuff
ruined, oh! I've got some paint on my new T-shirt. It's ruined.

"We know all about that, Sir," the inspector said. "The people in Swansea checked for us. The phone call from Norway only asked them about cars on the road now. That's why they didn't find anything. We soon found out about you and your MG."

Bishop turned to the children again.

"The police say you found a postcard. How ..."

"That's enough, Mr Bishop. We ask the questions here," the inspector said.

When the inspector's questions were finished, Paul had a question.

"Can we have a look at the Escort, please?" he asked.

"I don't see why not. Take them along, would you please, sergeant."

The inspector turned back to the children.

"Thanks a lot, kids, but don't do anything like this again, will you. It is **our** job, you know. And it could have been **very** dangerous. What if Mr Bishop had caught you in his garage, young man? A few seconds later ..."

They went out of the building and across to a big car park. They soon saw the Escort. A policeman was keeping an eye on it.

"These are the kids who caught Bishop," the sergeant said. "They want to have a look at the car. They've only seen it in a photo."

The policeman opened the doors. "Help yourselves."

Paul checked the front *passenger* seat, but he couldn't

---

passenger, someone in a car, train etc. who isn't the driver

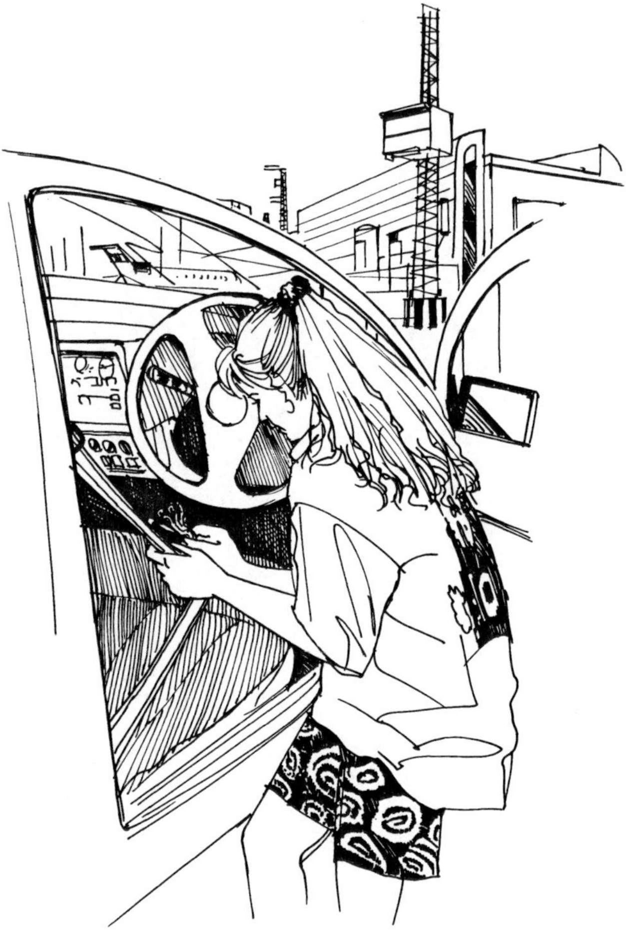

find anything. While he was doing that, Jackie went round to the driver's side of the car, and she looked, too.

Suddenly she pointed to something. "There, Paul," she said. "That's what you're looking for."

Paul came round to her side of the car.

"Where?"

"On the *safety belt*."

"What is it?" the sergeant asked.

"A little piece of blue wool," Paul said. "It's from Mrs Bishop's pullover. But why is it on **that** side of the car?"

"You're a great detective, Paul," his sister said. "Women drive cars too, you know."

---

safety belt, the safety belt keeps you in your car seat if there's an accident

Comprehension

Chapter 1

1. What is it like on the path?

2. The woman is worried because ...
   (How many answers can you find?)

3. What do the children see and hear?
   How do they feel?

Chapter 2

1. Can you tell the children's story so far?
   You can start like this:

   We were out in the boat.
   We paddled along the side of the fjord. Then we heard ...

2. Do they find anything on the path?

Chapter 3

Try to explain why two of the photos are interesting.
You can start like this:

The first photo shows ...
She's wearing ...
But you can't ...
The second photo shows ...
And you can see ...
One of them ...
Paul thinks ...

Chapter 4

1. Why did the murderer buy a newspaper?
2. Why would no one know he and his wife had been to Norway?
3. What would the murderer say to his neighbours? You can start like this:

   "Well, you know Jean and I ..."
4. Why is there something funny about the Escort?
5. Were there any clues at the Hotel Husum?

5

1. You don't think Paul is right. How could you answer him if he said these things:

   Paul: I think he drove down here.
   You: Well, he **could** have ... but ...
   Paul: Perhaps he stopped at a camping site.
   You: ...
   Paul: Well, he'd have to stop at a garage.
   You: Yes, but they wouldn't ...
   Paul: I bet he threw his wife's things away somewhere.
   You: But ...

2. What happened when the man in the Escort stopped at the second garage?
3. Say as much as you can about the piece of postcard.

Chapter 6

Look at the map of England.

1. Where do the people in the story live?
2. How far is it from one town to another?
3. How far is it from Dover to Bournemouth?
4. How would you get there?
5. Where do you think the Robinsons came off the ferry?

Chapter 7

Think about it!

1. Why **didn't** Ray Bishop drive off after the Robinsons?
2. Why **didn't** he throw the old number plates away?
3. Why did the policeman say, "this is something for the inspector"?
4. Why did the inspector shout, "Get me a car, and I need two officers"?

Chapter 8

Think about it!

1. Why do you think Ray Bishop murdered his wife?
2. Why does Ray Bishop's girlfriend say, "Ours, you mean"?
3. Why do they want to go to Rio?

4. Why are they so nervous?
5. Why does one of the passport officers say, "Go through the list very slowly"?
6. Why is Ray Bishop surprised when they catch him?

Chapter 9

Now we know.

1. Why was Ray's camera bag so heavy?
2. Why was there a photo of the car and the church?
3. Why didn't the Norwegian police find out about the number plate?

   ... and why does Jackie say Paul is "a great detective"?

www.easyreaders.eu